Imperfect Beings

Embracing the Light

Cynthia

aka Blushing Baketress

Grateful to the Words From The Heart writing group.
Your gifts are meant to be shared with the world.

Contents

Motivation

The words on the page could not stay any longer
The pronunciations sounded improper
But that's the mess needed to heal
Strong emotions, a deep reckoning that goes down smoother than
prescribed pills
The words could not stay, they had to go
Turned into butterflies to let the world know
That strength, knowledge, and power could not be restrained
That the biggest redemption comes from pain
The butterflies knew exactly where they were going
Nothing would stop this remedy from flowing
To the depths of despair
To breakdown hopelessness
They fly through the air
There's a cure coming forth and it was created in the dark
Where the beast left his mark
But that scar is where the beauty would begin
Through tornadoes and rippling waves of dirty sin
A monster of literature and words often left unspoken
Who knew this was the way to let the hope in?
Through her book of poetry came the greatest opposition of the lonely
The butterflies would carry the words to people who needed it
the most

The story that was told is "You're never alone"
For the Lord has made me whole
Come read what I've gone through
If He can do it for me
Surely He will do it for you
Jesus is the fix, the medication, the antidote
Now let me share with you the words that I wrote

Introduction...

In any relationship, especially in the beginning, you give your heart away willingly.

A heart that is shiny, new, healthy, and the brightest of reds.

Then the little stabs begin to happen. The piercings of broken promises, misunderstandings, expectations unmet, resentment, and unwillingness to forgive.

They start tearing small holes in your heart.

The funny thing is that sometimes the same people or situations that created the holes also sew them back up. They become an instrument to your healing.

They clean up the blood and apply ointment on the wounds.

It gets confusing...

These poems are about ALL relationships. Relationships between family, friends, and the lovers we choose to be in our lives. Mostly you will find, these poems are about the most important relationship we will ever have.

The relationship between ourselves and God.

What do we think about ourselves? Who does God say we are?

Do we value ourselves first so that we can have healthy relationships with others? Is our identity first found in Christ before we go looking for love somewhere else? Are we all trying our best to love ourselves first, then one another?

We're much more alike than we think. We struggle with similar thoughts, goals, and situations. Pain is something we can all relate to.

Sometimes we must walk in darkness scattering seeds of hope before we see a harvest unfold light into our lives. Trying to figure out who the world tells us we are and who we are truly meant to be is a daily battle.

One thing remains in all of this. WE are not alone. YOU are not alone!

We are ALL in this together.

We are ALL "Imperfect Beings."

The people who walked in darkness have seen a great Light; those who dwelt in the land of intense darkness and the shadow of death, upon them has the Light shined.

Isaiah 9:2 (AMPC)

Stuck in Deception and Darkness

Life

We're like the dog that starves at his master's gate.
Waiting and fearing to hear our fate.
Hungry for hope and feeling so faint.

We're like the lamp which has no light.
Ran out of oil, consumed by the fire.
Darkness lies still as a sheet, laid out to smother our desires.

We the living dead are a broken-down car.
We keep driving our minds insane,
not getting very far.

Playing the game of life.
Like amateurs,
we're still learning from generations past.
Yet taking every breath as if it were our last.

So close to fulfilling the lives that we seek.
Wanting to be so content.
Content like a pig devouring food in its trough.
All life could be gone,
with the quickness of a diseased cough.

Hopeless the weight that holds us.
Down the fate which pulls us.

Scattering Seeds in the Dark Valley

I am hopeful because God has great plans for my future. He lights up my path and directs me in the way I should walk. He is my almighty compass when I feel lost.

WAITING

Life is one big waiting line.
It spans out so far you forget what it is you're
waiting for.
And then there's the pit inside your stomach.
The hard piece deep in your lungs.
The feeling of "there's got to be more to my life, right?"
The unknown crushes you,
Leaving you immobile.
Like a zombie.
Going through the same motions,
and yet...
emotionless.

Why?
What?
When?
The frustration so strongly cries out!
The feeling of agitation so plainly written on the face.
The uncertainty of many undiscovered roads to follow.

What will come next?
Will it be better,
or yet just another fork in the road?
Another sign displays:
"Wait Here Please."

Do I cut in front of everyone?
No matter the cost?
No matter the fight?
Will I end up weary of a battle that leads
nowhere again?
...I can only say my famous phrase I have said millions of
times throughout the years...
"I don't know."

<u>Scattering Seeds in the Dark Valley</u>

I will wait patiently for the Lord. He
promises to renew my strength. I may
not have everything figured out but
God helps me endure and fills me with
wisdom when I ask for it.

The Days Are Evil

The days are evil.
The days are mapped out with time before I even wake.
Time stretches out like a drab lengthy rug.
Covering up leisure activities.

No time to spare!
24 hours!
Got to make my time count!

Oh, I do.
I do so much I can hardly stand!
Where's the time to sing,
to laugh and play?
Drink a hot cup of tea,
be with my love and my dogs.

Especially the time I need for me,
myself,
and I.
"You got to make it!"
I'm screaming inside!

I need to remain sane.
I need to be with myself and think.
I need to think about what I must do for myself first,
then what I will do for others.

I can't bury myself and forget who I am!
The days are evil.
Time is tick,
tick,
ticking away.

This day will never come again after night falls.
Can't fall behind,
got to get up and fill up my time!

Scattering Seeds in the Dark Valley

I'm going to make the most of every
opportunity so that no time is wasted.
I stay well-balanced in the blessed quiet
that God supplies for me. I don't stress
about my to-do list but I ask God what
He wants me to accomplish for the day and
He reassures me.

Lost

You're no good for me.
You take me lower and lower.
You come down hard on me.
When I think I'm doing right.
You tell me "Wrong! Wrong! Wrong!"

I try to stay strong,
but I am a failing soul.
Wounds cut deep,
brain out of control.

Looking for my home,
where I am accepted and loved.
I'm lost and nobody is looking for me.

<u>Scattering Seeds in the Dark Valley</u>

I believe that the Lord is my Savior and
there is no condemnation or guilty verdict
against me. I am made clean by the
blood He shed for me. He is my family
and I am never alone.

The Cloud

There's a cloud of distortion that follows me around.
It's dreadful, grey, and gloomy.
So full of heavy rain.
It showers over my joy parade,
It comes down hard.
With words of slander, it speaks:
"Liar,
no good scumbag,
you are dumb,
disgraceful,
you will never change."

It blurs my vision.
It warps my mind and tortures my soul.
With every purposeful thought of goodness that comes
to mind.
It plummets through to mutilate my uniqueness,
my individuality,
and my identity.
I'm left feeling unstable.

Sometimes I am aware of these misleading mind games.
Sometimes it is I who follows the cloud around.
I'm so used to tearing down my existence.
Tearing down my personality and branding myself as
someone else.

Forgetting my original name and design.
Losing track of the inheritance that is for me.
Losing track of the value and personal status that God
has marked me.
Marked me as one of His children.
I am unlike any other in the world.
I am special.
I am set apart.
I am His very own handiwork.

This cloud is a dark enemy that waits patiently.
Waits patiently to tarnish my worthy traits.
This masterpiece the Lord has created can easily be
overshadowed at times.
I get so distracted by the fog of disbelief of who I am.
My tears flow down my red dreary cheeks.

Every obstacle surrounds me,
and I feel fenced in.
Left bare naked for the words of criticism to cover up
my body with shame.
Whether I act right or wrong the outcome remains
the same.
Caught up in the abyss of my own mind games.

Scattering Seeds in the Dark Valley

I was created wonderfully by God. He
knew me before time and is pleased with
His creation. Even though I have made
mistakes, the old patterns have passed
away and I'm made new in my Father's eyes.
He continues to transform my mind day by day so that
every thought is pleasing and good.

Thoughts of Defeat

Feels like I'm going crazy.
Scream into my pillow.
Hit my head against the bed until I go numb.

So insecure, confidence lost and gone away.
Wake up another day,
where I mess up first thing in the morning.

Go to bed crying, wake up crying.
No one around me is happy or filled with joy.
No one can help me but myself.
Nobody likes me and I see it when I look in the mirror.

Try to smile but I am met with glaring eyes.
I will just leave you alone.
I will be dust passing in the wind.
A ghost living in the shadows.

Nowhere to hide from me.
Itching to drive far away and never come back.
Start over and be someone different.
Not me.
Not the failure.

Nobody wants me around.
I am the only one who can lift my spirits from the dust.
Sometimes people need help, but that won't happen
for me.
I desperately need support and kind words but all I hear
are thoughts of defeat.

Scattering Seeds in the Dark Valley

Although the world, people, and my thoughts try to knock me down, I am never destroyed or abandoned by God. With His help, I am victorious in the battle that wars in my mind. He is changing thought patterns and destroying the wrong mindset that I once had. He is pleased with me as I grow each day.

Won't Ever Be Enough

I kiss you.
You say you never get affection.
I give you material things.
You say you never get anything you want.
I am positive.
You say it's annoying to you that I look on the
bright side.

When I try so hard to give someone what they want or
what they crave, what they long for,
but they don't receive it, see it or feel it,
it makes me want to give up on everything.

But the thing is,
I love you naturally,
in my heart,
in my mind and soul.
So how can I stop?

I am stuck in the middle.
I never meet your true needs.
I won't ever be enough,
but I will love you with all my heart.

When I die you will think I never lived up to the friend
you expected me to be.

When I die,
I will think I tried every day to give you what you
needed,
to love you with my life.
But the love couldn't be seen or felt,
so,
in both our minds,
we will think the same.

That I was a failure.

Scattering Seeds in the Dark Valley

I know that everything I do is worth something to God. It is not useless. I am not a failure. God has filled me with His righteousness. My life reaps the fruit of His unfailing love for me. Not just in my life but with those I have a relationship with because God is so good to us.

REGRETS

Eyes feeling heavy and sunken in.
Thoughts of despair leave me bland.
Careless behavior sets in,
yet my mind is full of an emotional blaze of fire.
Heat sweeps through leaving my brain bare.
Can't concentrate,
can't think.
Dissatisfied with decisions made.
Confusion whispers "You're the only one to blame."

Scattering Seeds in the Dark Valley

I will cling to God in my confusion. I
know He is the Father of peace and not
disorder. I lay regret down at His feet
because with Him nothing I go through is
ever wasted. I can't wait to see how He takes
my mistakes and turns them into something beautiful
that will inspire others as well.

To: The Narcissist
From: The Guilty Ones

There is no other like you.
You are perfect and innocent
it's true.
Everyone around you is wrong.
Stay away before we ruin you once more.
Over and over we team up to throw our dirt on you.
To place the blame.
Nothing can ever be undone.
We can never live blameless,
like you have lived.

We are a big disappointment,
not uplifting.
We are destruction,
no foundation here.
We are scum,
not white as snow.
You know how to live right,
we are still learning.

There is no other like you.
A different species we've never seen before...
We will burn in Hell,
scratching at Heaven's door.
Useless.
Worthless.
Hopeless.
Guilty as Sin.
We are all in the same boat,
push us offshore.
Then we cannot hurt you anymore.

It will be like we never existed if that's what you wish.
But you never get your way, right?
Only we do.
We only please ourselves.

So, you are all alone,
we are the guilty ones and come into your life to bring
you pain.
All of us bring nothing but pain.
You never hurt us, we only hurt you.
Isn't that right?

Scattering Seeds in the Dark Valley

In Proverbs 21:2 (ESV) it reads that
"Every way of a man is right in his own
eyes, but the Lord weighs the heart."

I pray for mercy for myself and others.
I pray for God to destroy toxic patterns that put us
through emotional turmoil. Please search and test our
hearts until we are pure.

We must all appear before the judgment seat of Christ
regarding what we have done to others, whether our
actions are just or unjust.

Stolen

I feel like to you,
back then I was worth so much more.
In the early years before much was endured.

Then again... love has always been a struggle.
Once an excited welcome,
now turned to a low mumble.

Sticking so close together.
No one else in sight.
To become sick of each other.
No longer a delight.

Hard as hell to make it through.
Sacrifices made,
stolen the best parts of me and you.

Scattering Seeds in the Dark Valley

God fills me with His grace even as I suffer.
I thank Him that He restores me and my
relationships. I am steadfast and strong
through all situations. 

Switches

With day comes night.
With joy comes despair.
One minute in love,
then hate fills the air.

It makes me sick.
There's no peace or contentment.
Like a garbage disposal.
Just a flick of the switch,
intimacy goes down the drain quick!

Soon yellow turns to gray.
Adornment turns to disappointment.
Like the press of a button.
Switch to feeling GREAT!!!
To feeling like NOTHIN'!!!

Want to stay in the sunshine.
That bright warm feeling.
Instead, we've plunged into the darkness.
Plunged into the sweltering heat of anger's nonsense.

Just like that!
Quick!
Like a bat of an eyelash!
The serenity of silence switches to unwanted yelling.
Did one thing right but the relationship is failing.

How can I get to the other side?
To stay there and enjoy myself.
To be filled up with pride,
no self-doubt.

Not basing who I am on what you think.
I can be alone,
but I don't want to.
Good people are far and few.

Only if we work out these kinks,
Will we be set free?
Finding solutions is a wild mystery!

Wounded...hard to believe in good.
Hard to be who you think I should.

Scattering Seeds in the Dark Valley

I decide to make every effort to keep
unity in my household. I will think and
speak peacefully, humbly, and gently.
Sometimes I will mess up because I am
human. But no matter what I declare
that my house is built on love, not strife.

Another Disappointing Day

Another disappointing day.
The kind where you want to give up and get lost somewhere.
But have nowhere to go.
When you no longer want to explain, and you don't care if anyone gets it.
You thought it would be a super chill day,
containing nothing more than laughter and peace.
But the stars had something else in mind.
As they always do.

"Always" is a term used by the dramatics.
If I'm being drama-filled, I wish to be filled with peace instead.

I have yet to succeed in feeling that peace.
I still stir inside feelings of rage, displeasure, and torment.

It's one of those days when the one person who tells you they love you the most, is not even talking to you.
You know, because you had a stupid fight that was complete nonsense.
Yup, these days are the worst.

Just because I know we were supposed to laugh and
play today.
We were supposed to hold each other and kiss.
Now the night has fallen, and another loving
opportunity missed.

Scattering Seeds in the Dark Valley

With God's grace, I continue my efforts for
peace in all relationships. No bitter root
will grow in my heart. I have Christ's love
inside of me that I keep pouring out onto
others no matter how I feel. I act loving first
and then feelings of love will start to well up inside of
me until I can no longer contain them.

Mixed Emotions

Trying to look on the bright side,
but I swear it's me you despise.
I smile wide and try to look into your eyes.
Not even a cold stare do I get back.
Not even one glance my way.
Just the other day you swore you loved me, adored me,
would die for me.
Now I see a blank face before me.
I am deceived once again.
We're both missing out on what could have been.
Look forward and move on past the sins.
Please?
It won't be easy.

<u>Scattering Seeds in the Dark Valley</u>

God brings forgiveness and transforms
hearts. I forgive others just as my Savior
forgives me. He gives me the courage and
vulnerability to extend grace to others
without being fearful of the outcome or
rejection.

PARTS

You branded me like a cow.
One of your own.
Took the best parts of me to devour.
Threw out the rest.
Threw out parts that tasted sour.
Threw out parts too hard to swallow,
yet I continued to follow.

Part of your herd.
Part of your family.
Unruly at times,
but looked up to you like you were holy.

Trusting the one in charge of my life,
not knowing you would cook me up,
cutting for yourself the biggest slice.
I was scarfed down by you.
Piece by piece I filled you up.
You were so full,
the rest of me was thrown in the garbage.

I thought I was family.
I thought I was a friend.
Never did I think your adoration for me would end.

Scattering Seeds in the Dark Valley

I feel deeply hurt by my loved ones. In
these times I declare Jeremiah 17:14 (MSG)
"God, pick up the pieces. Put me back
together again. You are my praise!" He
hears me and comforts me. God is close
to those who have a broken heart.

Doing Right

I need a vacation from my mind.
Thoughts, worries, doubts, and reasoning all turn
into sobbing.
Burning droplets pour from my tired,
red eyes.

I thought I would be OK.
I thought I had made something of myself.
To sweep away regret and fear.
Fear of staying the same.
I'm no longer sane.
I'm no longer content.
I'm no longer feeling shiny and brand-new.
I'm no longer of value to you.

Instead, I'm feeling old in spirit and personality.
Weary, weak, and wounded.
Caring too much about what people think.
Trying to meet higher standards set before me,
yet falling short repeatedly.

I need renewal and restoration.
To be simple-minded and happy.
To be like a faith-filled child.
I feel robbed of what could have been.
I don't know how to move ahead in action.
I'm learning a lot,
but failing when tested.

Failing in the times when perfection matters the most.
I need a break.
To go far away.
To become a stable rock again.
To gather my thoughts,
so that my speech is understood when I speak out.

I desire to be tougher than this.
No more tears,
only action and strength.
I desire simplicity, peace, and clarity.

How I crave laughter and smiles,
yet I don't have enough joy to pour out.
I'm always trying to live RIGHT,
yet I'm continually led to believe that I am scum.
Just like the rest of 'em.
I'm no different.

I desire esteem and confidence.
I want to trust again.
At this age, I'm still needing to
reach these goals.
Goals that seem so far from my grasp.

I'm so close that I can feel the embers still burning.
A faint light brightening inside of me.
I'm ready to just "do."
I'm done with overthinking.

Questions remain in my mind.
Questions that pull me back.
Farther and farther away from my purpose.

What is it that I just do naturally?
What is it that I do without thought?
Is it anything good?
What is my passion?

Empty me out because I am so full of crap.
I need repair.
I need to do only RIGHT,
for a very long time.

Scattering Seeds in the Dark Valley

I'm going to keep believing that He has a purpose for me. I must fan the flame of the embers that faintly burn inside of me. He has a gracious gift and talent specifically made for me, just as He does for all His children.

MISINTERPRETATION

I speak and you hear blah, blah, blah.
You speak and I hear hate, hate, hate.
Words spewed up like a volcanic earthquake.
How long will this new argument take?
Fake it til' you make it,
advice I struggle to take.

Whom have you become?
Where have I gone?
Confused expression leaves us both withdrawn.
Oh, how I long for your understanding,
the conversations turned to silence is maddening.

Two people sewn together for years start to unravel.
Wish I could look up answers in a relationship manual.

<u>Scattering Seeds in the Dark Valley</u>

I look in my Bible, which is a manual to all
of life's questions. I find that it is better to
listen than to speak. I understand that
when it comes time to open my mouth
I will either speak life or death. I choose life.
Pleasant and gracious words will flow from my lips. All
confusion disappears and understanding is revealed to
me and others.

What Am I? I Am Disrespect

I am Disrespect.
I bring tears to man's face.
I bring dishonor and strife.
I am the blade that lacerates.
The three-cord knot of God,
of man and woman,
I erase.

I am rebellion at its finest.
Nothing comes together when I disrupt harmony.
And unity becomes a minus.

Sometimes with a small snicker or a roll of the eyes,
I come.
You may not even know I'm here
until the damage is done.
I make men walk with their heads held down,
full of discontent,
stripped of purpose and left to frown.

I conjure up thoughts of hopelessness,
leaving women stranded and alone.
Leaving them confused to the core of how they got here,
feeling ignored.

I am creative,
making all things a weapon of destruction.
Once a plate to feast on in union... now shattered into
broken pieces of sharp glass on the floor.

Don't bother with your opinion,
I have no ears to listen.
I only have a big mouth to interrupt.
People have no sense of what they speak of.

I am the King of good intentions.
I try to lend a helping hand but end up in ruins.

I self-destruct,
consuming all around me,
flickering flames that burn a perfume of bitterness.
The list of dissatisfaction is constant on my lips.

I speak death "If your God is real,
why does He allow you to fall for my dirty tricks?"
I see no change,
no positive account to report.
I'm filled with evil glee as I chuckle and snort.

I live to deceive,
and I am a master of disillusion.
You can't name me,
so,
I breed more confusion.

If only you understood and see what I do.
You would embrace change in your marriage,
then love would feel fresh and new.

You would show honor to your spouse,
treating them like a King or Queen.
I am more than mean,
I am rude and impolite.
I am ungracious,
speaking death,
defending my wrongs in every fight.

I am Disrespect,
a complete mess.
Strife and stress are all that is left.

Now that you know what I am,
be peaceful,
be virtuous towards your man.
Now that you know what I am,
be honorable,
willing to lay down your life for your woman.

Scattering Seeds in a Dark Valley

I thought my spouse should not be hurt
by something that wouldn't hurt me,
but that is selfish thinking. Everyone
is different. I can either tear down or
build up my household. I choose to build
it up by being respectful. I will listen, admire, show
understanding, honor, value, look up to, and submit to
my spouse. Although I am an imperfect being, God gives
me the skills I need to be a virtuous wife.

STRESS
CALLOUS
ANXIETY
REGRETS
SORROW

Stress,
how you've made me callous.
Hardened,
not feeling a thing.
But anxiety,
you live on and I feel you throughout.
Through my tears.
Through my memories.
Through my regrets.
The "if only's".

Is my face wet with tears?
A glimpse in the mirror shows me my sorrows are there.
I see my mistakes clearly,
if only I could see life more clearly.
If only I made better decisions.
I can start today.

That is about all I can do.
Or give up.
I choose to begin life again.
Over and over I will try.
I will wake up every day to a new hope.
Throughout the years,
the dark scars start to lighten.
My only hope is that what caused these scars is
forgotten.

Scattering Seeds in the Dark Valley

I hope in God who never lets me down. He
always comes through with everything I
need. He wipes away all regret, trauma,
and anxiety.
Every tear cried He keeps in a bottle because
He loves me so much.

Branded

You branded me instantly.
You thought I was just a farm animal, stuck inside of a
dusty barn and fenced in.
Your opinion of me was that I had no value.
You put me inside of an imaginary box that you created.
You didn't take the time to see how great I am.
The value and worthiness of my friendship was yours to
lose before it ever began.

Yeah, I might have been branded with a hot iron.
It left an identifying scar that reads 'Rejected''.
But any obstacle I face, through mistakes and
disappointments, I continue to use every ounce of
endurance to confront issues in my own life.
To grow from them.
I choose to not waste my strength to prove how
valuable I am.

For I know that you are the one that's fenced in.
You're watching me from afar as I freely live out my
destined purpose.
A destined purpose to fly and soar to greater heights.
Using liberty as my wings.
For I am an eagle, not a barnyard chicken who must
stay in their coop.
I am valuable.

But guess what? I humbly acknowledge that you are valuable as well.
That is why I long for you to put your opinions aside so that we could flock together.
With the risks I take comes much success and adds value to my life.
It's amazing to fly above the clouds in the sky.

But I will always carry a bit of sadness tucked between the pinions of my wings.
Because I know that as an eagle I must fly solo.

Scattering Seeds in the Dark Valley

God has stamped me with a seal as His very own and put His Holy Spirit inside of me as a great inheritance. This is an everlasting reminder of His promises to me.

To My Bad Thoughts!!!

Hey, bad thoughts!
You won't talk down to me anymore!
Make me feel rotten to the core.
Every part of me becomes pain and numbness.
All around me is a mess!

You won't make a joke of my hopes and dreams any
longer.
My need to succeed is growing stronger.

You need to listen to me.
And know that the bad-mouthing is done,
over!
I am here for you.
To cover.
To cover you up and throw out the doubts.
To straighten you out.
To make you whole again.
It's not the end.

It's me that holds me back.
I am what I believe in myself.
I am my own worst enemy.
I can't depend on anyone else to make me feel
differently.
It's my thoughts that limit me.

It's my voice that I hear.
It's my thoughts of fear.

Only I can be there for me.
Only I can change my life's trajectory.
By changing my thoughts.
I will fight daily.

Scattering Seeds in the Dark Valley

I make it a habit to overcome bad thoughts
with good thoughts. I win the battle in
my mind. I cast down all lies of deception
and darkness. I push forward to God's
light and truth and I find freedom.

Embracing
Light
and Truth

Love Again

I just want you to be nice to me.
Please just treat me kindly.
Love me for me.
Don't shut me out when you're having a bad day.
We could embrace each other instead,
make the most of it.
You see how the world is cruel and unjust.
How one moment you're here, then you're dust.
So why treat me this way?
Is it because the world has stolen pieces of your heart?
Is it because you were searching for those pieces in me, only to be
disappointed?
Is it because the pain became too harsh, leaving scars and marks
too deep to clean?
I know you're not this mean.
I know in your heart there is a longing to have compassion again
for mankind.
You will find this love again, inside of yourself.
You will see the man God sees and loves.
I will have my best friend back, and in me, you will see,
your true love again.

INSPIRATION

Love is patient and kind. Love is not jealous or
boastful or proud or rude. It does not demand its
own way. It is not irritable, and it keeps no record
of being wronged. It does not rejoice about injustice
but rejoices whenever the truth wins out. Love never
gives up, never loses faith, is always hopeful, and endures
through every circumstance.

    1 Corinthians 13:4-7 (NLT)

CAN WE TAKE TIME?

Time to relax, no fussin' or fightin'.
My head has been spinning too much.
Time for family, grins, and traditions.
To be thankful for what we have.
To let go of the past and embrace
hope for our future.

Please can we get closer?
Can we feel successful?
No more division.
Can we laugh and play?
It's time for my heart to stop
beating in frustration.
It's time for the headaches to go away.

Will you look for me?
Will you be what I need?
Time for togetherness.
Time to be one again because I'm done feeling...

alone.

<u>INSPIRATION</u>

Finally, brothers, rejoice. Aim for restoration, comfort
one another, agree with one another, live in peace;
and the God of love and peace will be with you.
    2 Corinthians 13:11 (ESV)

Don't Want To Be

I don't want to be broken anymore;
Your word says I am whole in You.

I don't want my value to be stripped away,
Your word says I am far more precious than rubies.

I don't want to be stuck in a pit of depression,
Your word says I am redeemed and powerful.

I don't want to be a peasant;
Your word says I am clothed in strength and dignity.

I don't want to walk in darkness,
Your word says on the solid rock I stand.

I don't want to feel robbed by the injustice of the world,
Your word says I am recompensed.

I don't want to walk on the crooked side of the road,
Your word says you make my path straight.

I don't want to make plans without You,
Your word says my steps are ordered by God.

I don't want to feel lonely any longer,
Your word says You will never leave me nor forsake me.

I don't want to bow down to any other besides You Lord,
Your word says I will become just like the idols I worship.

I don't want to live in sin,
Your word says the prayers of the righteous come to fruition.

I don't want to ever stop making my desires known to You,
Your word says ask and I shall receive.

I don't want to put my armor down,
Your word says to guard my heart, for it determines the course of
my life.

I don't want to stay selfish in my attitude,
Your word says to whom much has been given, much is required.

I don't want to be ungrateful;
Your word says giving thanks qualifies me to share in Your inheritance.

I don't want to pray "Lord could you just" prayers,
Your word says to come boldly to the throne of grace in my time of need.

I don't want to depend on myself,
Your word says those who depend on the Lord will be like a tree planted by the stream, forever yielding fruit.

What I do want, Lord, is You,
Your word says to first seek the kingdom and all other things will be added to my life.

What I do want, Lord, is to dwell in Your presence,
Your word says in it, I will have full joy.

What I do want, Lord, is to be transformed each day into Your likeness.
Your word says in my morality, I will see You face to face and be satisfied.

INSPIRATION

And I know that nothing good lives in me, that is, in my sinful nature. I want to do what is right, but I can't. I want to do what is good, but I don't. I don't want to do what is wrong, but I do it anyway. But if I do what I don't want to do, I am not really the one doing wrong; It is sin living in me that does it.
    Romans 7:18-20 (NLT)

What We Deserve

You are a heavenly dream come to life.
Even though this reality is filled
with strife.
You manifested from a sweet
hope found inside.

Everything good, innocent, and
lovely.
You can't ever be ruined by the cruel jokes of this world,
so ugly.

Feelings of disappointment were not meant for us.
But love, prosperity, faithfulness and trust.
This is what we deserve and we will make it happen.
In the end, we will be the ones laughin'.

All that has been invested,
how could we not become happy?
Winter passes, yet all seasons still feel crappy.
Some things we cannot control,
rage, and despair roll in to make us unfold.
But we can't let it!

You are strong!

I am optimistic!

We're still on the straight and narrow, although it looks so twisted.

You say you cannot handle anymore, but I know that's a lie.

Don't you get it?

With this bond, no hopes, no dreams can diminish!

Let's keep running until our purpose is finished.

INSPIRATION

Two are better than one, because they have a good [more satisfying] reward for their labor; For if they fall, the one will lift up his fellow. But woe to him who is alone when he falls and has not another to lift him up! Again, if two lie down together, then they have warmth; but how can one be warm alone? And though a man might prevail against him who is alone, two will withstand him. A threefold cord is not quickly broken.

Ecclesiastes 4:9-12 (AMPC)

Suitcase of Dreams

Today I tore up my suitcase of dreams.
It was all I could do to let off some steam.
In my mind, I felt oppressed.
I cried out, "God pull me out of this mess!"
Had become obsessed with overthinking.
Stressed beyond reason.
Depressed by the blustery season.

The muscles in my forearms were tired.
Carrying around dreams, it seems, that had expired.
Could I get out of this rut?
Just garbage my life's work?
Would I glance in the trash with regret, thinking I'd been a jerk?

Took a couple of deep breaths, somehow feeling peace and relief.
Got off my knees, pulled up my sleeves, and shook the dust off
my feet.
I noticed the suitcase of dreams was torn but still locked and held
together.
I lifted it up, no longer a heavy burden, it felt light as a feather.
I had mustered up some strength from my Heavenly Father.
I stood up feeling 10 inches taller.

A soft voice spoke, "God's gifts and His call are final."
By His word, I was able to walk another mile.
And as the minutes went by,
I no longer wasted time caught in despair.
I knew that the will of God would always be there.
He does not change His mind about those to whom He gives
His grace.
A shining smile replaced the pain on my face.

It is written for me. He sends His call.
Clenching tight to my suitcase of dreams, I stumble, but I will never fall.
Unalterable, set in stone, and permanent.
I must admit, I forgot to believe my life is a testament.
His call I will firmly achieve.
All the hopes and dreams He has for me, are far more than I can conceive.

I sat still and pondered, had I really learned the lesson?
Was there more to this anger and second guessin'?
He told me my anger was justified, wasn't right to keep the dreams inside.
To carry on my own with no one to share.
Such a fallacy and so unfair.
Uncontrolled emotions had not gone to waste.
Through a crack in the suitcase, shined His perfect Grace.

He exposed the insides, the truth now lay open.
It's you Oh God, I put my hope in!
Now the dreams that were once locked away, move on and prevail each day.
What an adventurous journey that lies ahead.
For those who tear up the suitcase of dreams, choosing to live them out instead.

INSPIRATION

For God's gifts and His call are irrevocable. [He never withdraws them when once they are given, and He does not change His mind about those to whom He gives His grace or to whom He sends his call.
   Romans 11:29 (AMPC)

Anew

Tear out my insides and make me anew.
Take every part of me and replace it with You.

Make me the woman You so desire me to be.
I'm clenching tight to Your Holy garment childishly.

I wait in anticipation as You create a stable place of peace,

where I can rest my heavy head and feel at ease.

Stir me up, so I'm head over heels for You.
Generate a desire within me,
to put You high up on a pedestal.

Be number One in my life because I cannot breathe by myself.
I have failed so many times when I've left You dusty on the shelf.

My concerns and distress have caused mayhem to abound.
I must confess that I need You around.

Settle the current, disentangle the bondage, free me of the pain
that's held me hostage.

Walk with me through the narrow path.
Hold me up as I weaken in my stance.

Guide me past twisted branches and murky water.
Tighten the grip on Your faithful daughter.

When I have lost all senses, no longer feeling You in my presence.
Support me, give me eyes to see with Your spiritual lenses.

A new day is drawing near.
Redesign what I thought was true.
When I look at myself in the mirror,
confidence will brightly shine as living proof.

That You were here all along.
That it's not just me left here to believe.
That You're something I can feel and someone I can see.

You in all Your glory, manifested inside my soul.
I have committed all to You.
You have taken full control.

Your promises are here, materialized in the land of the living.

Not just in my dreams or in a book,
but out of the heart, You're giving.
It's up to me to take another look and keep on believing.

I lift up Your name Jesus and hear You cheering me on.
Now the thread-like path doesn't seem as long.

Obstructions are gone and faith stands forefront.
I'm headstrong.
I may be tarnished but never bent.

The words You speak bring life.
With You, I stand on high.
To all my broken dreams, I wave goodbye.

INSPIRATION

So all of us who have had that veil removed can see
and reflect the glory of the Lord. And the Lord -who
is the Spirit- makes us more and more like him as we
are changed into his glorious image.

    2 Corinthians 3:18 (NLT)

Balance of Dreams

It's all a balancing act.
I step lightly but with a sense of urgency.
Moving from one position to the next.
I start to stress over my performance.

At the end of the day, I'm faced with the question.
Was I good enough?
Did I fall short of my Lord's expectations, my husband, family, or friends?
Did I match up to the woman I said I wanted to be?

I feel like I'm being pulled in numerous directions.
My time is torn to shreds by mundane tasks or never-ending to-do lists.
I'm trying so hard to find purpose while washing dishes but have an intense pull in my gut.
A strong sense tearing me apart.
I feel that my purpose is so much more.

I'm trying to move forward in life.
I'm trying to leave regrets behind, but they claw up my legs and lay rest in my mind.
It's a battle to not be dragged down into that dark hole of mistakes.
I must resist the thoughts that speak
"There is no time left for my success, dreams, or passions."
Trying not to be selfish but my soul screams out "What about me?"

Constantly creating balance, routines, and goals.
I've become an expert at reading self-help books, yet I fail with a discouraging heart when I don't see the results I long for.
Putting my trust in God, that He loves me, that I am what He says I am.
Walking upright, with a smile, head held high even though I don't feel like it.

Wondering where I have gone, the silly girl, fun, carefree, fearless, confident, and bold.

Taking in deep breaths adjusting myself to be mindful,
but just rushing through another week.
So many things I must do and then there are the things I long, desire, and WANT to do.
When my spirit calls within me, begging for my time, it pleads "Don't forget you are more!"

Now if I could only get this balancing act together.
Maybe before I have it all together, I can reach inside and pull out my creative dreams.
As long as I live, they are within reach.
Dreams that require me to be even more of myself.

This time it will be what my heart desires.
No overwhelming feeling, no burden, no tumultuous thoughts.
No doubt or shame of what could have been.
This time, a content mind.
Stable, and with peace.
This time, I will be ready.
This time, I will do it.

INSPIRATION

For I know the thoughts and plans that I have for you, says the Lord, thoughts and plans for welfare and peace and not for evil, to give you hope in your final outcome.
   Jeremiah 29:11 (AMPC)

And I am convinced and sure of this very thing, that He who began a good work in you will continue until the day of Jesus Christ [right up to the time of His return], developing [that good work] and perfecting and bringing it to full completion in you.
   Philippians 1:6 (AMPC)

Hardheaded

Learnin' lessons got me stressin'.
Ouch! I stay hardheaded.
Got a hard heart too.
Willing to lay it down for you.

Shed my old skin.
Fly like a butterfly.
Division keeps me stranded here,
we can't see eye to eye.

Day in, day out I try to keep the peace.
I stay light on my feet.
Take your hands and shout "Dance with me!"
"Give me a kiss!"
Doing anything I can to dismiss,
this depression and frown.
Smiling hard, swaying hips,
longing to feel your love come down.

In my vision, I see the life that could be,
love and respect for eternity.
All hands on deck for this love that has no end.
Calling out your name,
"Can I see your delighted face again?"

An expression of joy,
planted on that handsome head of yours.
Craving to be wrapped in your arms
to smell the essence of your pores.
My wits are disarmed, and I lose my mind once more.

Left here reaching for your heart,
seems like an untouchable grasp.
Praying so hard,
my head spins so fast.
Becoming a prisoner of hope,
I'm hoping this love will last.

INSPIRATION

If possible, as far as it depends on you, live at peace
with everyone.
 Romans 12:18 (AMPC)

What leads to strife (discord and feuds) and how do
conflicts (quarrels and fightings) originate among you?
Do they not arise from your sensual desires that are ever warring
in your bodily members?
 James 4:1 (AMPC)

And Still

I wake up, I praise your name, constant in Your word, waiting for
change.
Struggling, feeling like a target to my enemies.
Standing on the word that's kept humans grounded for centuries.

Listening although Your voice sounds stifled.
A deception of lies stays fixed on my eyes, a blindfold.
I keep asking You to shape and mold, but when I hear Your word,
I can't even do what I'm told.

I'm caught in between two different worlds; my mind is confused,
and my thoughts are all swirled.
I take the step of faith only to fall back down on my face.
I come back to You and ask for more grace.
Boldly I come, I know You see that I'm trying,
But how much longer do I fall?
Feels like I'm dying.

Sometimes I wake up with tears in my eyes, visions so blurry,
thoughts of demise.
If I can't get it right, will You accept me, nonetheless?
Feeling stressed, an all-consuming mess.
Lord! Is this just another test?
I am obsessed with ugly thoughts and left with no reason.
Is this just another passing season?
Set a table before my enemy, condemn the ruler of treason.

I have been lied to, betrayed, left to doubt, to be afraid.
And still, I wave my hands in the air.
Calling on Your name in Heaven, my soul left bare.
The enemy taunts that "life isn't fair!"
And still, I look to Your word and realize You're there.
Peace comes from praising You, thoughts become clear.
I muster a smile, glowing from ear to ear.

I get sent through this wave of emotion.
I scramble for a lifesaver, caught up in the ocean.
Arms flailing wildly, heart paralyzed and frozen.
Numbness sets in, and still, I call out Jesus' name.
Situations must change!
Thoughts need to be tamed!
Take away my shame!
I believe You are the same.

The same God who calls out and loves His creation.
The One who declares victory over nations.
The King of Kings, The Redeemer, The Restorer!
I stand before You, and still, I cannot let go.
Pull me close dear God, fill me with hope.
Trusting You for justice, move swiftly on my foes.
You cover me with peace, anointed oil,
from my head to my toes.

<u>INSPIRATION:</u>

If you need wisdom, ask our generous God, and He will give it to you. He will not rebuke you for asking. But when you ask Him, be sure that your faith is in God alone. Do not waver, for a person with divided loyalty is as unsettled as a wave of the sea that is blown and tossed by the wind.

    James 1:5-6 (NLT)

You prepare a feast for me in the presence of my enemies. You honor me by anointing my head with oil. My cup overflows with blessings.

    Psalm 23:5 (NLT)

Sit and Wonder

Sitting here in bed wondering how I got this man.
What did I do, nothing deserving I am certain.
But somehow, here you are, beside me every night.
Touching me with strong arms that wrap around my belly.
Sturdy hands that sweep over my face.
Gentle as silk but more stable than the eagle's grip.
I feel safe and secure, my heart is mended by you.
I'm engulfed in your sweet love.
Submerged in the smell and taste of you.
There's never a time that I don't want more, yet I am satisfied
without a doubt.
I cannot control myself, all my wits dissolve with a single kiss.
And I sit and wonder.
Is he thinking of me too?

He sits in bed and wonders how we came to be.
What was it that she saw in me and wanted so badly?
His body surrounds her like a fortress at night.
He caresses her soft skin and runs his hands through her curls.
Her delightful fragrance fills the air.

How did I captivate her so easily?
Why did the first glance from this woman instantly mean forever in her heart?
He's determined to give her the world ever since she picked him out of the crowd.
Her kisses are refreshing like a cold spring of water in the desert.
So satisfying and yet he can't get enough.
All his worries dissolve.
He can't help but sit and wonder.
Is she thinking of me too?

INSPIRATION

Like an apple tree [rare and welcome] among the trees of the forest,
So is my beloved among the young men! In his shade I took great delight and sat down, And his fruit was sweet and delicious to my palate. He has brought me to his banqueting place, And his banner over me is love [waving overhead to protect and comfort me].
   Song of Solomon 2:3-4 (AMP)

Proverbs 17:22

A cheerful heart is good medicine, but a crushed spirit dries up
the bones.
Reduced to dust and left on my own.
For these sins, I cannot atone.
I gasp for air as I weep and moan.

Lord fill me with peace, I am full of disease.
This pain has torn me apart, to say the least.
In my mind, I escape to a place where I prosper.
I let go of this painful monster.
If only Your grace I can foster.
I will walk in a confident posture.

I pour these cheerful hearts down my throat and I hope that I
can cope.
I smile without a doubt.
Passions on fire, no longer burnt out.
The doctor has no clout.
It's You Lord that has erased my pout!

Consume me and don't leave me alone.
Breathe life into me as You did in the Valley of Dry Bones.
Don't You know that I need You!
I long for good news.
Tattered and bruised, losing grip as I slip in these shoes.
Walk around confused, expecting You to infuse, Your inner
strength and grace.
I cannot refuse.
Thank you is all that's left to say.
I won't be dismayed.
Your love is continuous and never fades.
A cheerful heart was prescribed to me today.
I'm popping these pills until my crushed spirit goes away.

INSPIRATION

A happy heart is good medicine and a cheerful
mind works healing, but a broken spirit dries up
the bones.

    Proverbs 17:22 (AMPC)

No Longer A Mystery

You and I could be,
living my fantasy.
My fantasy man.
Lover of my life.
No other like you,
makes me smile.

When I first saw you,
you were a mystery to me.
I knew I wanted you right away,
but I didn't know why.
I glanced your way and caught your eye.
We shook hands and said "Hi!"
What was it about you?
Little did I know,
I would get to see just who you are,
and what you're about.

Started as a flicker in my heart.
Butterflies in my tummy.
Began as a mystery.
I picked you,
now you're kissing me.

We talked for hours on
the phone.
Listening to your voice,
your life, and all the funny jokes.
I got to see beyond
those sweet brown eyes.
The amazing parts of you
that were hidden inside.

It's funny how two can come together.
We didn't know
a thing about each other.
It took time to unfold
this magical mystery.
I picked you and
now you're kissing me.

<u>INSPIRATION</u>

So they are no longer two, but one flesh. Therefore, what God has joined together, let no one separate.
Matthew 19:6 (AMP)

Vital Love

A vital necessity.
To reach out, to pray to Thee.
Finding the gift of life You bring.
Purposeful You created this woman to be.
I need You so desperately, entirely.
You alone can complete me.

A vital necessity, the Holy Spirit who dwells in me.
Make me whole again, renew and refresh Your spirit within me.
Open my eyes to see the one You claim me to be.
The one You call by name, the one You paid a high fee.
When You died for me, Your love poured out so openly.
How I yearn to realize, all the value, the worth You've
placed in me.

A vital necessity, my tears cry out to Thee.
Speak life into me with peace that flows through You
abundantly.
Needing to feel like I'm living triumphantly.
Your power came alive from the moment You created me.
Fearfully and wonderfully made You sing over me.
Overjoyed that I was born, Your beautiful baby.
Adopted me as Your own, My Father, You love me.
Unconditionally, unmatched, never leaving me.

A vital necessity, I cling to Thee.
A new creation, You have conceived in me.
Thank you, all praise to Thee.
On eagle wings, I fly freely.
You renew my life so effortlessly.

<u>INSPIRATION</u>

Then you will seek Me, inquire for, and require Me
[as a vital necessity] and find Me when you search
for Me with all your heart.
    Jeremiah 29:13 (AMPC)

God's Positioned Queen

This is to you, My Queen.
Don't loosen your position.
Hold tight and fight toward the mission.
The battleground is bleak and you feel all alone.
In My presence, I pick you up and place you on My throne.

To hold dear, to hold tight, you are precious, one of a kind.
Not only in My sight, My little girl, but for all the world to see.
Your inner glow shines bright in this desolate place,
your charm as vast as the sea.

Pick up the pieces, and dry your eyes.
For your shame and broken heart, for your mistakes and ill fate.
I give you the prize of My love to replace all hate.

This is to you, My Queen.
Don't loosen your position.
You have seen with your own eyes, victory over the opposition.
Face the facts, don't you dare turn back.
You know through it all I have held you up on high.
With every sigh, with every cry, it was Me that filled the void
inside.
These are the facts and I do not lie.
You My lovely are the apple of My eye.

For I made you, I know what you're capable of.
Unconditional love, but a savage heart of a warrior.
I stand before you, in this no man's land you're no foreigner.

Here for a purpose.
Remember without Me you're living aimless.
Stay connected My daughter.
I promise you'll see more than what's on the surface.
My heart beats for you, I have not forgotten My sweet child.
Watch Me move, quieting thoughts that have run wild.

This is to you, My Queen.
Don't loosen your position.
Stay engrafted in Me.
Open your ears and listen.
I repeat.
Don't loosen your position.

INSPIRATION

The Lord (God) says to my Lord (the Messiah), Sit at
My right hand, until I make Your adversaries Your
footstool.

   Psalm 110:1 (AMPC)

But you will not even need to fight. Take your positions;
then stand still and watch the Lord's victory. He is with you, O
people of Judah and Jerusalem. Do not be afraid or discouraged.
Go out against them tomorrow, for the Lord is with you!

   2 Chronicles 20:17 (NLT)

A Soldier

The butterflies in my stomach try to keep me paralyzed.
I must shed my old skin.
I realize there is a warrior within.

I believe that God sets me higher than my enemy,
giving me the power to slay this foe.
I have the victory,
the Lord will never let me go.

I stand with Him on my side,
to be transformed.
He keeps me alive.
My almighty Father whispers "Vengeance is Mine".

In my weakness, I lean on Him.
He takes these filthy rags of sin.
I am His princess,
clothed in beautiful armor.
Glistening strong,
a woman of valor.

What the enemy has stolen,
has been made good in God's hands.
On solid ground,
now I stand.

For You have made me a soldier.
I have mastered the battle in my mind.
Your plans bring victory right on time.

I speak out your word,
my tongue is a sword.
In demolishing the evil one,
I find my reward.

INSPIRATION

Therefore, put on every piece of God's armor so you will be able to resist the enemy in the time of evil. Then after the battle you will be standing firm. Stand your ground, putting on the belt of truth and the body armor of God's righteousness. For shoes, put on the peace that comes from the Good News so that you will be fully prepared. In addition to all of these, hold up the shield of faith to stop the fiery arrows of the devil. Put on Salvation as your helmet, and take the sword of the Spirit, which is the word of God.
    Ephesians 6:13-17 (NLT)

Perfect Father

When I had no father,
You adopted me.
Told me I was Your daughter.
You'd look after me.

With all the enemy has stolen, I felt robbed from within.
But God, You took my bitter heart,
given me a glowing countenance again.

You have taken my story.
I'm restored and renewed, in awe of Your glory.
My eyes see Your truth.
The good path laid before me.

I'd be a fool to not believe that You care for me.
Forever for me, never my enemy.

Never make promises that You cannot keep.
Forever my number one fan when I feel defeat.

The heart of a Dad who's love is unconditional,
even as my mistakes are made habitual.

My hero who saved me since the day I was born.
Who knew each word I would speak,
before I was formed.

All the days of my life,
You hold me tight in Your arms.
You whisper words of affection,
leading me away from harm.

I bask in Your goodness forevermore.
My perfect Father, who I so adore.

I will follow You all my days.
I will strive for Your image of perfection,
as I learn all Your ways.

I cling to You in my deepest despair.
When I'm crying out "Abba Father, help me!"
You are always there.
Thank You for being my first and last love.
I trust that one day, we'll hold hands in Heaven above.

INSPIRATION

For all who are led by the Spirit of God are children
of God.

So you have not received a spirit that makes you
fearful slaves. Instead, you received God's Spirit when
he adopted you as his own children. Now we call him,
"Abba, Father." For his Spirit joins with our spirit to affirm
that we are God's children.
Romans 8:14-16 (NLT)

My Warrior, My Knight, My King

My Knight in shining armor.
To you,
respect, admiration, and honor.

You hold your shield up high.
You protect your family and walk with a powerful stride.
Adversity daily you must fight.

The soft, loving, and caring parts of you stay reserved for me.
The harsh, rugged, and manly parts of you ward off attacks
from the enemy.
Pulling the life force out of them.
In an effort to protect me.

You're a wise King,
loyal in speech and action.
Your daily victories bring nothing but satisfaction.

A man of your word, and full of integrity.
God's favor will surely follow you daily.

In this life, true blessings will abound.
Swift vengeance and justice for all our enemies around.

You're smothered in blood and sweat,
looking out with a furrowed brow.
You are covering all bases watchfully.
No point of entry for foes do you allow.

You're just a human being,
trying to live life right.
God sees every effort you display,
day and night.

You're wounded and tattered,
because you are a mortal man.
You're doing your best, but the rest is in His hands.

My Warrior, My Knight, My King.
You're all of these things because on Him you lean.
I'm grateful He put you on my team.
I will always be your adoring Queen.
Now, let's kick up dust as we run to our dreams.

God is marching before us and I am running beside you.
To fight.
To struggle.
To laugh.
To live victoriously.
Every day in your arms, you have blessed me!

I am proud to call you my lover.
I speak anointed prayers as thick as oil to cover.
To cover us from all danger.
To cover us from the crooked path.
To cover us from evil plans.
Because you are my man.
I trust you.

Your visions lead us to a flourishing land.
Impossible for us alone,
but with Him, we can.

INSPIRATION

Likewise, husbands, live with your wives in an understanding way, showing honor to the woman as the weaker vessel, since they are heirs with you of the grace of life, so that your prayers may not be hindered.
  1 Peter 3:7 (ESV)

For the husband is the head of the wife even as Christ is the head of the church, his body, and is himself its Savior. Now as the church submits to Christ, so also wives should submit in everything to their husbands.

Husbands, love your wives, as Christ loved the church and gave himself up for her.
  Ephesians 5:23-25 (ESV)

Greater love has no one than this, that someone lay down his life for his friends.
  John 15:13 (ESV)

YOU REIGN

Because of who You are.
YOU REIGN
Because You are the Counselor, the Keeper of tears.
YOU REIGN
Because You shed Your blood to cover my sinful ways.
YOU REIGN
Because You see the best in me no matter what mistakes I make.
YOU REIGN
Because Your loyalty and peace are constant, unchanging.
YOU REIGN
Because You are as strong as an Ox, yet as gentle as a
butterfly kiss.
YOU REIGN
Because You tell me no when I need to hear it, and yes just in the
nick of time.
YOU REIGN
Because You're Holy, Your DNA bleeds out love in a world that is
tarnished.
YOU REIGN
Because You're no respecter of persons, a glorious predestined life
is available to all who believe.
YOU REIGN
Because You use the foolish things of the world to shame the wise.
YOU REIGN

Because Your ways are marvelous. What is impossible to man is
possible for You.
YOU REIGN
Because You are the King of Kings and the Lord of Lords.
YOU REIGN
Because of Your wisdom and great inheritance for Your children.
YOU REIGN
Because I can count on You to hear all my prayers.
YOU REIGN
There is no other like You. You can never love me more than you
do now.
FOREVER LORD.
YOU REIGN

<u>INSPIRATION</u>

Then I saw Heaven opened, and a white horse was
standing there. Its rider was named Faithful and
True, for he judges fairly and wages a righteous war.

He wore a robe dipped in blood, and his title was the
Word of God.

On his robe at his thigh was written this title: King of all kings and
Lord of all lords.

Revelation 19:11, 13, 16 (NLT)

Unchanging Love

You are living waters.
Flowing through my veins.
Keeping me alive.
You refresh me.
You restore me to a greater existence.
Flowing waters travel through my body.
I am consumed with Your love.
Your love is unchanging.

You are my father.
I am Your child.
With my head held down in shame, You take Your hand, gently tilting my chin up.
You meet me eye to eye.
There is no condemnation.
No words of defeat or disgust spew out of Your mouth.
You tell me I'm Your most prized possession.
Your love is unchanging.

You are a sturdy rock.
I stand on You as a solid foundation.
I climb upon You to get to the secret place.
I hear You whisper sweet words to me.
As the world comes crashing down, this rock remains unshaken.
My stability and fortress of protection.
Your love is unchanging.

You are an eagle.
My soaring hero.
You swoop down and rescue me from the pit of death.
You fly me over roaring waves and still the ocean.
Once again, I am surrounded by Your living waters.
I breathe in a gust of fresh peace as it fills the air.
Your love is unchanging.

I prayed for You to lead me.
You rolled out a new script for my life.
I was in pieces.
My body was weary.
I was dragged across a floor of despair for way too long.

I was barely breathing.
I was holding onto Your promises to keep me alive.
Knowing You had more for me.
Knowing not to cover up in shame.
You pursued me all along.
You are forever in love with Your creation.
You called me by name, back to Your loving arms.
Your love is unchanging.

INSPIRATION

Even youths shall faint and be weary, and [selected] young men shall feebly stumble and fall exhausted; But those who wait for the Lord [who expect, look for, and hope in Him] shall change and renew their strength and power; they shall lift their wings and mount up [close to God] as eagles [mount up to the sun]; they shall run and not be weary, they shall walk and not faint or become tired.

Isaiah 40:30-31 (AMPC)

He who believes in Me [who cleaves to and trusts in and relies on Me] as the Scripture has said, From his innermost being shall flow [continuously] springs and rivers of living water.

John 7:38 (AMPC)

Proud Papa

Hit the gas!
Hit the gas!
Gonna' take you for a ride.
Hit the gas!
Hit the gas!
Gonna' make you feel alive.
Hit the gas!
Hit the gas!
Let out what's inside.
All your dreams run wild,
when you believe in Me, My child.

You passed all the tests again.
Pleased with you I am.
You tip the scales,
You score above 10!
I sing praises over you, My daughter.
I am overjoyed to be your Father!
I never leave My sheep to be slaughtered.
I spoke out loud to the enemy:
I taught her!
Taught her to rejoice in her sufferings!
Taught her to call upon My name!
Taught her to speak greatness into existence!
Taught her to have no shame!
Now it's time, My daughter, to be led.
Full speed ahead!

Hit the gas!
Hit the gas!
Gonna' take you for a ride.
Hit the gas!
Hit the gas!
Gonna' make you feel alive.
Hit the gas!
Hit the gas!
Let out what's inside.
All your dreams run wild,
when you believe in Me, My child.

Listen to My Way and follow Me.
Never dismayed, if you allow Me.
Allow Me to pull out of you,
the treasure stored up within.
No longer gravitating towards sin.
Hold onto Me tightly.
We're going for a ride,
it might get bumpy.
But it's fun and shocking.
Trust me, I will do all the talking.
They may mock you.
They may laugh.
They may tear you down,
and cause you strife.
But remember I gave you My life
so that you could live your own.
Live up to your potential.
All real, nothin' superficial.

Hit the gas!
Hit the gas!
No braking.
No yellow lights where you are going.
No seeds to be sowing.
Harvest, favor, retribution,
2-fold blessings.
Completely proud Papa,
of lessons learned through My testing.

INSPIRATION

After you have suffered for a little while, the God of all grace [who imparts His blessing and favor], who called you to His own eternal glory in Christ, will Himself complete, confirm, strengthen, and establish you [making you what you ought to be].
   1 Peter 5:10 (AMP)

The Lord your God is in your midst, A warrior who saves. He will rejoice over you with joy; He will be quiet in His love [making no mention of your past sins], He will rejoice over you with shouts of joy.
   Zephaniah 3:17 (AMP)

Dear Regret,

It's been a wild ride.
God knows I have tried
to please you.
I've pushed through
doubt and fear.
Used progress as a way
to make my thoughts clear.
But what is fulfilling about success
when you still naw at my intellect?
Leaving me stressed.
My mind like bone
in a mutts mouth you grind.
You hungrily rip away the present time.
I'm left with only my grimy past.
Whittled down to nothing
but rigid cells and mineral.
How can I last?

Utterly exhausted
trying to earn my worth and value.
Confusion is all I feel
when I'm around you.

Moving on to a greater perception.
Desperate to break away,
you were such a hard lesson.

Lord knows I have tried
to get in my car and drive.
To speed far far away
just so I could survive.

Wanting to shed you like amphibian skin,
but your shadow lingered around
like Unforgiven sin.

No matter how far or fast I sped away.
No matter who the new me
I decided I'd become,
when I arrived at my stay.

I would see your reflection in the mirror
"Thoughts of regret closer than they appear"

I can't take it anymore!
I need you out of my life!
No more fogging up my psyche.
Wearing me down
until I can no longer fight?

That's not gonna happen.
I've come to the realization,
I'm at my wits end.
To my soul I must tend.
This is the last time you will hear from me.
Logically, I now see.
That you are against me.

Like a childhood blanket I kept you close.
Not realizing it's myself I should be proud of the most.

You are not my friend.
You are far from a lover.
You are my enemy.
You were living undercover.

You almost got the best of me.
So I say farewell,
so I can become the best me.

No longer yours faithfully,
I'm leaving you behind.
Satisfaction within myself is what I find.

Philippians 3:12-14 (MSG)
I'm not saying that I have this all together, that I have it made.
But I am well on my way, reaching out for Christ, who has so
wondrously reached out for me. Friends, don't get me wrong: By
no means do I count myself an expert in all of this, but I've got my
eye on the goal, where God is beckoning us onward-to Jesus. I'm
off and running, and I'm not turning back.

Sunflower

I was the discarded one.
The one called failure.
The one ridiculed with harsh words,
that cut deeper than any weapon.
Words stabbed the very core of me,
until there was no more of me.

I remained lifeless and disdained.
I was torn into shreds by people You created.
People who were supposed to accept and love me.
People who were supposed to see the good in me.

Instead, they threw stones at me with bad intentions.
To destroy my identity.
To make me feel small
and lesser in value.
To fill me up with the ugliness
that they felt for themselves.

What they did not know
is that all those hateful words were like dirt
being thrown onto a seed.
A seed that would grow and sprout from the ground.
A root that would develop quickly.
Being watered with the very spit that came out of their mouths.
What they did not know is,
I would bloom into a Sunflower.

A Sunflower driven so deep into the Earth,
that I could not be pulled out.
Every time they walk by,
they cannot help but look upon my beauty.
They adore my grace.
They are filled with peace
as they gaze upon my yellow vibrant petals.
Even the imperfections impress them.
They wish they could be as stunning and upright as my stem.

But only One can pick me out.
The only One who took my hand,
and lifted me off the ground when I needed to be saved.
The only One who made sure the ugly words
did not turn me bitter.
The One and Only.
My Maker and Creator.
My Lord Jesus.